I Am Your Fa

By

Darrell McEwen

To My Wife and Yet to be Born First Child
Love Always, Always Love

Preface

To my unborn child,

I am your Father (you will become very familiar with this famous movie quote). This is my journal through which I will share the story of how you came to be.

You will meet some people along the way, you will also hear how your Mother and I came together, got married and decided to increase the size of our family by choosing to have you.

We will talk about sex, disagreements, arguments, drugs, depression, anxiety, stress, failure, success, happiness and love. Fair warning; you may want to skip a Conversation or two if you do not wish to hear about your Mummy and Daddy getting their 'bow chick a wow wooowww' on.

Your Mum may well disagree with some of the facts but it's not her story, it's mine.

Lesson: Never let the truth get in the way of a good story

For the sake of this journal I will call you 'Bean'. This story is being written for you. I have started writing this story the morning after Mum told me that she was pregnant with you. It is currently September, 2017.

The first few Conversations have been written retrospectively. The rest have been written in real time since I was told of your pending arrival. Just like '24' with Jack Bauer... real time! This series will still be ace when you're of age!

PS: You're due date is May 7th... I'm secretly hoping you're born on May the fourth ; you'll understand soon enough my small Padawan.

Conversation 1

In the Beginning

THE YACHT CLUB

You're Mum liked me... a lot!

The Yacht Club was a well-established bar here in Dubai but has recently made way for another 5* hotel along the marina walk. Because drinking here is expensive, expats more often choose to socialize in places that at the very least have 2-4-1 deals on drinks.

On a perfectly warm February evening I decide to go out for a few drinks with my friends and quite quickly find myself sat in front of 2 (perhaps 4 or 6) perfectly chilled beers. My friends and I have even managed to score a table outside which is unheard of at post work drinks on thirsty Thursday.

As the evening progresses it becomes clear that I am the target of a very attractive blonde lady that is standing by the entrance talking with her friends. It's important to note here that your Dad has zero skills in the 'chat up' department. I mean I am seriously useless, so bad in fact that I can't even fucking 'wing man' with any great effect. Basically, I'm a bloody dickhead when it comes to knowing when women are interested in me and trying to talk to them in a social setting is an unmitigated clusterfuck. Ask any of my mates and they'll tell you the same thing.

However, your Mother's intentions were made clear even to me when she invited herself to sit down next me and 'chat'. Well, she was doing most of the chatting while I was just happy to, probably not so slyly, perve at her boobs.

What is interesting here is that within that conversation I explained to Mum that I was leaving Dubai and heading off to Australia to start a new life in the next few months. That didn't seem to distract her from her mission, so we continue.

As the night goes on we do a bit of bar hopping, doing shots and listening to our friends make giant twats of themselves in the alcohol induced belief they are the second coming of Freddy Mercury at the Karaoke bar where we are warned several times to stop pashing/snogging in public. FYI: Public displays of affection are not allowed in UAE.

So Bean, this is where it gets interesting. It turns out we live down the road from each other so we decide to share a taxi. The taxi journey conversation invariably turns towards 'where to first?' I went up for coffee ☺

THE DEAL

Given the fact that my plan is still to relocate to Australia your Mum in all her wisdom comes up with a plan... a deal of sorts. Let's be 'friends with benefits'. This is clearly a winner with me and I quickly agree to the terms. Your Mum is gorgeous, she's a wonderful lover and we live 5 minutes from each other... no brainer, right?

LOVE

Now, apart from my obvious physical attributes your Dad is a caring, generous and loving man by nature and is an excellent cook. I assumed all guys are the same... your Mum tells me that they most certainly are not (a few frogs have come and gone her way). Soon enough your Mum is overwhelmed by what I have to offer and starts to fall in love with me. At this particular time, I didn't feel I was at the same point... I am a slow learner. Your Mum quickly corrected that.

A week or two later and over a few bottles of wine on the balcony your Mum expresses her emotions to me and asks me if I feel the same. I knew deep down that I did but for some stupid reason hadn't considered saying it out loud. Sure enough she dragged it out of me... 'I do fucking love you Susie!' (Just you wait, she'll do the same to you!) It wasn't so hard to say but I objected to having it drawn out of me so my response was more curt than lovey dovey. What a dick your Dad is!

Lesson: if you love someone, tell them.

Another lesson: learn to cook and be excellent at it.

(The way to both a man and woman's heart is through a well-cooked meal and a nice bottle of wine... flowers and chocolates are for amateurs – be sure to make a fab pudding).

So now 'friends with benefits' is out the window and we're in love and living together. What the shit just happened?!

Now I'm about to hit the fast forward to the wedding and the time leading up to it. It's about 2 years... hold on.

Conversation 2

More Love

I proposed to Mum on 1st November 2014. This was my second attempt. Which, incidentally, was the very day your cousin George was born and the same date your Great Grandfather (Mum's Grandad) proposed to his wife of 60 years.

For my 40th birthday Mum took me to Goa for a week... it was amazing! Prior to that I had gone to Cara's at the Gold and Diamond park to get a cheap ring, I was travelling abroad after all and didn't want to lose an expensive one.

On one of the evenings I identified my chance. Mum was going to go white water rafting the next day so I was going to have one of the pergolas all fancied up with flowing satin sheets, roses and of course champagne. So, my plan of action is already in my head thinking I was Don fucking Juan the super romancer of women the world over. I woke up in the morning excited about what the coming day was going to hold but there was a problem... the only thing Mum loves more than a glass of Rose is a bottle of Rose, then perhaps another... bottle. Mum does not deal with hangovers very well. She cancelled her white water rafting plans and along with it scuppered my plan. She fucked it!

Conversation 3

'Shall I Come Off the Pill?'

The wedding was great and when you're old enough we'll probably bore you with the 1hr 20m video. About 20 months ago Mum says to me 'Shall I come off the pill?' Me and Mum have always wanted children so we agree this is the best course of action. After all Mum has been on the pill since she was a teenager and it takes a while to flush all the chemicals out.

The first few months were fine as we weren't really trying to get pregnant. More like we weren't actively trying to stop it from happening. A few months pass by and we decide to actively try and become pregnant. Me being a very sensible man, I suggest we go and get checked to make sure we're both healthy and there are no problems. As I'm the boss, Mum agrees.

We make an appointment to go and see the fertility specialists and Mum has her 'bits' examined, blood taken and sent to the lab for checking. It turns out there was a small problem as Mum has polycystic ovaries... I had no fucking idea what that was either. The only thing I really knew about it was that a few of our friends had the same. Turns out it's not that big of a deal and more than a few women have this condition. I think Mum was a bit more stressed out about it than me... she's a stress head. This you will learn for yourself Bean.

Now my turn... the only thing I'm told is no ejaculating for 3 days before the appointment. Fine, I can do that. I've gone through longer droughts... much longer! So, I've seen different scenes on the TV about this situation. There's either porn of the TV, dirty mags on the side and sometimes a hot nurse came in to give you a lap dance to get you started. Fucking brilliant, let's go! Yeah, no. Bean, it was nothing like that! I get my name called and sheepishly I get up and go with the nurse. I knew what I was here for, she knew what I was here for and it made me more than a little uncomfortable.

The nurse leads me to a room and pretty much throws me a plastic container and a brown paper bag to put it in with the instructions 'please note the time when you "finish" For fuck's sake... OK then! This is where it gets very shit, very quickly. I walk down the corridor following the nurse, there's people on both sides of the corridor and I'm still holding my small brown paper bag. To my horror she points to the public toilet and says 'in there'. Oh My God! That's right, I have to now stroke one out in a public toilet with people right outside... no pressure! So, I proceed to knock out the quickest, stealthiest wank of my life.

The result, over 90M little sperms which is considered in the safe zone. However, 'mobility' was a few percentage points down. That's just the amount of healthy sperms that are well formed and can swim well. Apparently a third of them are shit anyway and are of no use for baby making.

We've now had our checks, got our results... let's get to making a baby. This is going to be the most romantic, dreamy and emotional baby conception in the history of mother fucking baby making. Hmmmm...

Conversation 4

Let's get Serious

About 12/14 months ago we decided to actively start trying in earnest to get pregnant. Mum got the mobile apps to know when her fertile window was – we quite literally stopped recognizing the Roman Calendar widely accepted all around the world and reverted to the 'fertile calendar'. The one where days of the month mean nothing, weekdays and weekends are irrelevant but days 10-18 of the fertile calendar are ferociously blocked out and under protection from all outside influences for baby making. To help in this process I was also on supplements which are basically anabolic steroids to sperm while Mum was taking a cocktail of pharmaceutically recognised supplementation as well as some Eastern medicine concoction that I'm pretty sure contained bark dust, pickled deer penis, unicorn horn shavings and dragons' breath.

Me: 'I need to pay Du by the 17th... What's the date today Susie?'

Mum: 'Day 9!'

Me: 'Cheers. But what's the other date?'

This went on for some time. And it got seriously stressful... like pressure was mounting. I would start to have internal panic attacks as day 10 was approaching. How did I know day 10 was approaching? Because I was told, that's how.

Without going into to much detail there was frustration under the pressure of making sure I finished. There was a lot of lube being thrown around as foreplay was a bit too much under these pressured conditions. 'Foreplay?' Fuck that, just get in to it boy. There was sweat. There was blood. Holy shit... there were even high 5's when we'd strung a few consecutive days together in the fertile period. A far cry from what both your Mum and I were expecting this moment to be.

A moment of sanity came when we agreed to just chill the fuck out! We both went off our respective supplement regimes and just enjoyed being in each other's company whilst paying more attention to the Roman Calendar and less on the other, although there was one eye firmly on the fertility schedule for certain.

The result was we started to enjoy the process (the sex!) more and the last few months have been great. Mum changed doctors and we're far more comfortable with her than the last one. Jesus Christ, I could only understand every third bloody word from the last one.

Not so long ago Mum made an unscheduled visit.

Conversation 5

Poppy Seed

On Friday 1st September, 2017 Mum comes in the bedroom at early o'clock and announces that she's pregnant by shoving a piss soaked stick in my face. My response; 'of course you are!' Mum had been symptomatic for a week or 10 days... some of it I'm sure she made up in her head from reading the many, many, many blogs, FB pages, Instas and magazine articles all of which seems to contradict one another. Most of it's full of wankers giving their uneducated opinions adding fuel to the fire of uncertainty that I'm sure most first time pregnant women experience. But, her boobs were aching so she must be preggers right? Not the first time I'd heard this BTW.

Of course, it was the most amazing news I had ever heard. I had a bit of a tough time expressing it that Friday morning as me and Mum had been up late the night before smoking fags and getting on the smash. We like to spend the occasional evening this way although I suspect those evenings may appear less frequently going forward.

So Mum trots off to the doctor to have the definitive test... it's always better coming from the doctor and not webmd.com or even worse 'google MD' FFS!? The result... No definitive answer yet, we have to wait for the blood test results. This is pissing me off now.

Finally, the time comes. I'm in my first day at my new job, I've already contacted Mum about 4 times during the day to ask if the results are available knowing full well she will call me immediately... but I ask anyway.

Mum rings me and proudly announces that the result is '299'. Yeah I know... WTF is '299' and are you pregnant or not?! She quickly follows with that means I'm pregnant – 299 is a hormone they test for to determine pregnancy. I don't remember what that hormone is and quite frankly I don't give a shit. Yes, we're pregnant and you are on your way!!

You are currently the size of a poppy seed. Basically a few cells resting against Mum's uterus.

The only people who know (as you are just 5 weeks old) is my Mum, Mum's Mum and Dad and Mark and Linda as well as Daisy and Rai. You'll get to know Daisy and Rai pretty quickly as Daisy is having baby number 2 a month before you're due to exit. Daisy and Rai are your Mum and Dad's beer buddies.

The interesting thing is Rai and I were out one evening celebrating the fact that Daisy was pregnant and I told him 'I am absolutely certain that Susie is pregnant'. I left it at that and we carried on drinking. Fucking Nostradamus I am!

Conversation 6

Apple Seed

You're now coming up to 7 weeks kid. We have our first scan together tomorrow morning to see how you're getting on in there. We're pretty pumped about it. I just hope when the doctor says 'there, can you see the baby' I can actually see something and don't end up looking like a 2 year old trying to find fucking Wally.

Mum leaked the news to someone extra over the weekend – Katy. She didn't even ask me if it was OK to do so. You see, we had previously agreed to consult each other before telling anyone and she goes and blurts it out within the first 5 minutes of having breakfast with her! I was pretty dirty I can promise you that. However, on reflection I know it's hard... like really, really hard to keep the news that you are on your way to ourselves so I let it go pretty quickly. I have wanted to tell so many people because I'm so excited.

I was out to dinner on Friday with Steve and Sarah (you'll meet them too – they're also part of the inner circle) and asked Mum if I could tell them. She said yes, so I did. They're both stoked for us and I feel relieved for having told someone at last!

The only symptom Mum is really showing is a need for sleep... whenever she can get it... all the time! I think she's actually looking forward to having more symptoms so the whole situation becomes more real... like 'holy shit! We're having a baby!!' real. I was sure she was going to talk herself in to having morning sickness. She literally told me every day that morning sickness is due to start in 3 days, 2 days... tomorrow. (These bloody mobile apps!) There were 3 or 4 calls of 'I feel a bit nauseous, this might be it – I'm going to be one of those that has morning sickness'. And if I do that means it's going to be a boy according to an 'old wives tale'. Panic over... I don't think you're causing Mum any sickness. Now I'll look like a right fuckwit if she ends up being sick every day!

Conversation 7

170bpm!

Holy shit! What an amazing experience. We went to the doctor yesterday to have a quick scan and see how things are progressing. Our very first photo of you and it was every bit as exciting and incredible as I thought it would be.

So we get to the doctor's surgery and I go in as Mum is running a little late. The traffic at Trade Centre is an absolute joke at peak time. If you end up being an expat brat you'll come to understand what is possible and what is not around peak times in Dubai. FYI: If it turns out that way and you do become an expat brat I will have your Mum slap the expat brat out of you. Some of these spoilt, entitled little wankers here need an old school clip around the ear (some of them even a closed fist to the face)!

Apologies, I digress... we go into the consulting room and sit down. Behind the doctor I can see this enormous machine in a dimly lit room. Mum goes in first to strip down as this is an internal type of 'activity'. Then we see these 2 distinct formations one is the 'food pouch' for want of a better description which feeds you as the placenta and umbilical cord are yet to form and the other is beautiful you. And if I look closely I can see your heart fluttering at 170 beats per minute! That has to be close to the speed of a humming birds wings flapping furiously while it takes a long drink of nectar... rapid AF!

Me and Mum then go and have a quick coffee and gush over each other about what we've just witnessed... the growth and development of our beautiful baby Bean. Everything is as it should be and you're just over 6mm long and we have had to adjust the approximate date of birth to 11th May 2018. I think Mum more so than me is somewhat relieved or at least less stressed as it is becoming much more real to us now. Because Mum has no real symptoms of pregnancy except sore boobs and the need for a lot of naps this exercise provides us both with a bit more reassurance that yes, we are indeed having a baby!

Oh yeah, we sent the black and white still photo to your grandmothers and I'm pretty sure they both almost exploded in a fit of joy. Daisy and Rai are excited by the snap as well but not as much as your Grannies... bless them x

Conversation 8

Wild Raspberry

You're now about the size of a wild raspberry. Your hand is about the size of a biro pen dot. Your spine continues to grow and your eyes start to develop... it's in Mum's app so it must be true.

While we were at the doctors last time they took a bit of blood to run some routine tests. On Friday just gone Mum got the results from the lab with the doctors notes: everything is fine, everything is normal, there's no need to worry about anything at all – or something to that effect. At the time Mum got the results I was at rugby... Oh yeah, I coach rugby as I'm too old and a bit banged up from a lifetime as a player. I coach 3 Women's 7's rugby teams at Dubai Sports City RFC – we did very well in 3 friendly games by winning all three games and only leaking 1 try across all games. This was rather pleasing as we had done a lot of training on defence over the previous weeks.

Anyway... Mum sends me a Whatsapp saying she has received the results and has just emailed them to me. So when I get a minute I reply 'for the love of God DO NOT Google the results'. Her reply 'too late, I already have'. FFS! (*hand slapping my forehead emoji). And guess what? The doctor was right all along!

I obviously had a few beers after the game. They were pretty tasty and I was knocking them back until I get this message from Mum 'So you're staying out all night then?' In case you don't know this is Mum code for 'I'm bored, I'm not enjoying not being able to go out, I'm not a fan of my own company anyway... please come home'. To be fair I'd had enough so off I trot to get a taxi home. The conversation was a bit murky but I do remember having some good chat and was told I was very cute the next day – result!

Speaking of the next day... poor Mum had a bit of breakdown. She's suffering from a bit if cabin fever... well actually a lot of cabin fever. At this point it's tough to go out socially because you have to keep this amazing secret that you really want to tell everyone you know – and a few strangers and all. The lying and misdirection is exhausting especially as its people you know and care about and most of whom know the struggle we had to get to this point in the first place.

The 'breakdown' itself was a bit comical. It went a little like this:

Mum: 'Organise something for us to do, I've cabin fever and want to get out of this fucking house!'

Dad: 'How about this?'

Mum: 'Ok, let's do that'

Mum: 'No, I don't want to that anymore'

Dad: 'Ok, let's go to the cinema to watch The Kingsmen'

Mum: 'Ok, let's go to the cinema'

Dad: 'This is where it is and when it is' (I had a specific window)

Mum: 'No! I don't want to go to that cinema

Dad: 'But that's the only time it's on'

Mum: 'I don't care'... followed by a few tears then everything was fine.

All the above took place over about a 9 minute period. It seemed like longer and I thought it was going to take longer. Thankfully it didn't and I think we went to see The Kingsmen the following day... it wasn't as good as the first one. Sequels are shit.

Conversation 9

No More Lemon Water

You're coming up to 9 weeks now Bean. I forget what size comparison that is for now. Mum clearly hasn't been on her apps to keep me fully informed. I'm obviously not able to do that for myself whilst I'm writing these very important entries for you☺

The weirdest thing happened the other day... every morning I make Mum a tasty mug of warm lemon water. It's part of my morning routine: get up around 6am to walk Rusty (your soon to be BFF), before going out I neck a pint of warm lemon water, come back and have a cuppa, feed the dog, make breakfast for myself (Mum isn't getting up at the moment she's sleeping a little more while you're baking) then take Mum up her lemon water... well, not anymore! After years of it she's decided that she doesn't like it anymore – hahahahaha. Saves me a job!

Next week we have our next visit to the doctor. We're to do this thing called a panorama test. A similar thing is done at 12 weeks to check that you don't have Downs Syndrome. What we're doing is having this panorama test a little after nine weeks which tests for the same thing by using DNA and... it can also let us know if you are a boy or girl Bean. Mum is completely undecided if she wants to know... I definitely want to know. It's likely Mum will win that discussion but I'll keep you posted.

BTW, these tests are a bit fucking nerve racking. I mean, the chances of any abnormalities are absurdly low but dark thoughts start to creep in to your mind. Anyway, we crack on.

Conversation 10

The Test

Firstly, a correction. It's not that Mum didn't want the lemon water it's that she didn't want the pinch of sea salt in it. I should have known better. After all I have become quite the Jedi and my powers of persuasion and mind reading are developing nicely – not bloody quick enough though. I'm considering going to the dark side.

On Wednesday we had our appointment with the doctor to do this panorama test. Obviously we had another scan and it looks as though you're developing quite nicely. You're a shade under 3 centimeters long now. We can see your little arms developing... in all fairness you look like a cross between Alien and T-rex. You were wiggling and moving around shaking your wee t-rex arms about the place and your heart rate was still topping 160bpm.

Once all the cool stuff has been done (the scan basically) we get down to business. 'Would you like to know the sex?' the doctor says. Mum looks at me like she doesn't know what I want... to reiterate, I want to know. Mum can be a silly sausage sometimes and asks me the same question 2,3 or 4 times just to check that I haven't changed my mind – I rarely have... silly Mum! So we end up going back and forth a few times before the doctor decides 'why don't I check the box that says find out sex and you can decide any time you like if you'd like to know.' Seems reasonable... we agree and move on. Secretly I'm just like 'just tick the fucking box lady!'

Mum is doing great and still doesn't really have any symptoms of pregnancy except for being a bit more tired still. So the scan came as a bit of a relief to see you squirming around in there. Mum has started following this fitness model chick on Instagram who is 14 weeks I think – she's pretty hot and hardly got a bump. Mum loves her, hates her, compares herself to her, wants to be her, and wants to stab her in the face for her shit smug updates... I think she's going to 'unfollow'.

Went to another brunch this weekend for Rai's birthday and had to pretend to be drinking booze again. Not too long to go with all this bullshit lying, deception and misdirection... it's really starting to piss me off.

The master plan I think has been dealt a fatal blow... we were planning on telling friends that we were expecting you on my birthday this coming weekend as we expected to have the test results back. But we won't have the results for 3-4 weeks. Bollox.

Conversation 11

The Results

Right then... there's been a long wait but the results are finally in and they are as clear and definitive as can be. Are they fuck!? What we got was a list of what I assume were chromosomal markers for developmental disorders and alongside them was a probability marker... like 1/12,000 and another column which suggested the 'safe zone'. After Mum did a bit of googling and explained it to me all was fine and the results in fact what were we expected – normal. If there had been any issue with anything I'm sure the doctor would have called us in. We have another scan/doctor meeting on Wednesday (day after tomorrow) so we can ask our questions.

FYI: if you ever have any questions about anything, ever – ask your mother. If Google ever handed out certificates, awards or even doctorates related to Google use she would crush the universe of Google users. True story!

So now it's out there... people know we're having a baby. No more impossible secrets, military-type urban evasion techniques or outright bullshitting. Thank God!

The very next day I had rugby training in the morning... a very hot Friday morning. After all the shit I've spoken about how rubbish this secret is to keep I forgot that it was OK to tell anyone. Twat! So then I was chatting with some of the senior ladies team once training had ended and the conversation came around to the kids coaching (which happens just before the senior ladies train) and then realized I could openly say that we were going to have a baby... OMG! There it goes... 'Oh, by the way girls, my wife and I are pregnant with our first child'... and that was it. I mean, I'm a low key kind of guy but the seemingly and overtly lack of enthusiasm and excitement at what was happening almost went unnoticed! I know this handful of girls reasonably well as I see them more often than I see some of my friends, such is the coaching commitment, but I felt like I had to build up a little bit of courage to even say it out loud. What a fucking anticlimax.

On Wednesday the doctor is bound to ask us: 'would you like to know the sex?' Mum is still swaying between wanting to know and wanting the Hollywood moment of me proudly announcing your sex to her once you're out... 'Do you want to meet your new son/daughter?' I'll still love you if you watch these bullshit RomComs distorting perceptions of real life – but I won't stop ripping them apart as you watch that utter garbage.

Standby....

Conversation 12

Barry

It's agreed, we're going to find out if you're a boy or a girl. The list of pros has seemingly outweighed the cons. I'm so excited and massively anxious as I meet Mum at Starbucks before our appointment last Wednesday (it's Monday now). Half way through my halloumi and zatar wrap Mum walks in and announces 'right, we're going to find out the sex.' Immediately I shit myself at the thought of finally knowing if you're a he or a she... it's another step in the many reality checks I've been getting the last few months.

It was such an easy process to find out if you're a boy baby or a girl baby... was it fuck!

After the formalities are taken care of at the doctor's office which involve an internal scan – which is amazing, checking Mums BP and taking a urine sample we're sat down and Mum pops up 'we've changed our minds and would like to know the sex. If you could please tell us that would be great'. Doctor: 'I don't know the sex'. Oh FFS!!! I've been building myself up to hear this information. I am so close to the edge of seat my fat arse has nearly gone too far forward and your answer is 'I don't know'. Bollox!

'What do we (you) need to do to find out and how long will it take?' They only have to send the request to bloody America who did the test for chromosomal abnormalities. The answers we're looking for will be with us in a few days. Err, excuse me, what does that mean? Tomorrow? Friday? Are you even open on Friday? If you are open are you rostered on? Oh god! #palmtotheface

Friday rolls around and we find ourselves at Daisy and Rai's compound pool with Otto giving it large at his swimming ability. He's bloody good too! It casually comes up that we asked about the sex at our last meeting at which point Daisy has a burst of action and excitement and proudly suggests (tells) 'ring them, ring them now!' Mum says 'I don't have the number sav...' 'I have it, I have it here on my phone' announces Daisy. Mum and Daisy have the same doctor, you see. Mum starts ringing... Rai has the video on us... I'm once again (you guessed it) shitting myself... after we get through the menu, press '1' followed by '#' for blah blah blah.. doctor is off sick today but we'll email you and/or phone you. Piss off, I don't want to know now! Jokes – of course I do.

Now, there were a few issues with Mum's contact details but anyway Mum calls me midway through Sunday and says 'I've got an email from the doctor but I haven't opened it as I want to do it together' I whole heartedly agree and can't wait till home time. The anxiety is building all afternoon. I walk in, drop my kit bag, pat the dog, kiss Mum... 'Right then, let's open this bloody email – I'm shitting myself'. Drum roll please...... we open the email with breath abated... Oh no! Not again!!! It's a fuckin email confirming that we want the results emailed to us. I storm off upstairs to get out of my work clothes in a right strop!

Mum then decides to email them back saying 'yes please, email them to us' then she heads off to boot camp. She's been doing very well at keeping her exercise levels up, making me very proud. At this point I'm a bit dejected about the whole thing and crack open a beer to console myself while I prepare dinner. Mum gets back and says she's got an email reply – OMG, I wasn't expecting this. I haven't had time for the anxiety to build or shit myself. 'Shall we open it?' she asks. To which I respond... well, I'm sure you can imagine my response. She whips open the attached document – little did I know she knew exactly where to look on the report. Before I'd even had a chance for my failing eyes to identify the first word 'IT'S A BOY, IT'S A BOY, IT'S A BOY!' Oh. My. Word. I will now stop calling you 'Bean'... you are now 'Barry' until further notice.

Finally I am put out of my misery... never mind all the political correctness, gender role expectations load of BS...you are a boy... you will be my son... you will become a man... you will be the head of our family one day... you will be its protector and you, my son, will be spectacular.

Conversation 13

Avo

I finish my morning routine, walk upstairs and step over Rusty who is waiting patiently at the top of the stairs to assume his position at the end of the bed – he's been in full protection mode with Mum recently. I barely get through the door and 'Do you want to hear about Barry? He's 15 weeks?!'

So, you remember I told you Mum has all these Apps and stuff that give out updates... well today you turn 15 weeks old and probably unsurprisingly you are about the size of an avocado. One of your Dad's favorite foods!

The highlights are your bones and skeleton are forming and you can flex and extend your arms and legs. Perfect for the next phase where we can start to feel you kicking. Your heart is also in full development mode – you're going to need a strong ticker if you're to last the full 80 my son.

The only other thing of any interest to report is that Mum had her first pregnancy related day off work today. She didn't feel well at all. Don't fret though kid, she's a tough girl and has shaken it off this afternoon.

Oh yeah, on Wednesday night (day after tomorrow) you will be making your first international flight. We're off to England (which will be your second favorite rugby team - #sorrynotsorry) to see Emma and Jamie get married. I

reckon your Dad is going to thoroughly enjoy their hospitality
– cheers!

Conversation 14

It's a 'Seppo' App

As predicted, I thoroughly enjoyed the hospitality. Maybe even a little too much as Mum and I nipped off a wee bit earlier than closing time. Obviously I blamed the night flight that I hadn't fully recovered from... it may have also been the 2 hours in the mansion 'anxious drinking' champagne. Whoops!

So that was your first international trip little man... how about it?! We also got a taste of what it's going to be like to travel with you... a baby. Fuck! All we bought back was a push chair, albeit a bloody nice push chair (it's cheaper to order online in England and get stuff sent to Grandma England's place). There were way too many questions surrounding how we were planning to return to Dubai with it and for the first time in probably forever I have to actually use one of them airport trolleys. I reckon Mum is already fretting about travelling to England over the summer with you... that's why she's getting Grandma over for a while – so she can assist with the journey.

In other news, we're moving to a bigger house in a few weeks. A nice 3 bedroom gaff with maid's room (storage!). Mum nearly wet herself when we walked in... 'I love it, I love it, I want it, I want it'. This will be your first ever house. I hope you like it!

This app that Mum uses is clearly an American app when she describes your growth updates to me every Monday morning (Seppo... Septic Tank... Yank... American!) as you're now the size of a dill pickle. How bloody big is a dill pickle? Fucked if I know either! I assume slightly bigger than an avocado. The 2 things that stuck in my mind from Mum's regular Monday chat were that you should be starting to hear things now... cue the classical music downloads – Grandma NZ reckons Baroque is the one that's going to make you a clever clogs. I'll save you a long winded explanation... Google it! The other thing was that you may start kicking. Although I doubt that will be for a few weeks yet as Mum's stomach muscles are clearly good and tight and she's hardly showing a bump yet. She's an athlete!

One last thing before I sign this one off... in England we had our first bit of 'panic'. Mum sneezed in the night and it produced a pretty sharp pain in the side of her stomach... it's all OK though as it was just a sign of the connective tissues starting to expand around her tummy. Although in future she should sneeze sat up and ideally with her legs together... the danger is later down the track she might pee her pants. #funnynotfunny #gladmendonthavebabies

Conversation 15

Sweet Fanny Adams

There's nothing too dramatic to report in your development wee man. We had our first external scan with you last week – to be honest it looked just the same as the internal one before that. The doc was scraping over Mum's belly to try and get a butchers at your organs to give them the once over. 18 weeks is a little early and it's normally done at 20 weeks and it seems a lot of development occurs in just 2 weeks. Apparently you need to fatten up a little (not some creepy reference to Hansel & Gretel) as the scanning technology responds better and more accurately with some body fat. Eat up kid! You're growing well... strong and long legs by the looks and we even got a peek at your willy. There's something rather satisfying in receiving further confirmation that you are a boy... like DNA wasn't enough. Yep, I can be a dickhead sometimes. So, there's Sweet Fuck All going on with you but... over to us.

Mum and I have a lot going on right now. We're pretty much committed to getting a business going selling 'nursing rocking chairs' with all the added extras like ottomans, blankets, pillows etc. I'm also trying to find suppliers in China for 'Time Out' stools that have a built in 3 minute timer for when kids are little shits and don't listen to their parents. I'm sure you'll get some time on yours... I'd be disappointed if you didn't try and push the boundaries at least a little. We'll be encouraging you to push all the boundaries you can as you grow up but we'll also show you how to be clever about it. Otherwise you just end up receiving exactly what you don't want and end up looking like a bit of an arse-hat.

We move to what will be your first ever home on Saturday – the day after tomorrow. Welcome to stress town... population me. Fuck it! Just to move out of JVT and in to Arabian Ranches we have driven all over bloody town – about 23 times to collect paperwork, signatures, stamps, pay deposits, have one deal fall through to then agree terms with a new place across the same road. (Some wank puffin property owner that probably got an extra tenner a month – I hope his tenants make a mess of the place and stain the kitchen cabinets with curry powder. That smell never comes out!)

Our front room currently looks like the inside of a shipping container... a shipping container that has fallen off a truck, a truck taking a hairpin turn going 110kph, rolled down a cliff flipping 48 times and smashed in to another shipping container... I can't stand the mess and clutter. Did I mention your Dad has a touch of OCD about him? Sorry in advance for that – it pisses your Mum off sometimes too. In any case it's all about to sort itself out over the next few days.

Your first gaff is much bigger... a 3 bedroom + maids room. Now then, it's quite common in Dubai to have help. Generally speaking that comes in the form of either a live-in or live-out nanny. Your Mum and I have always been of the opinion we would like live-out help. Turns out that's what most of our friends with children thought as well... they all have live-in nannies. Gemma and Barney dropped that little nugget of information on us last week... let's see.

I've really got to get my fat arse in the gym. I'm sure there are going to be plenty of photos taken on the big day and I must do something about these man boobs and spare tyre around my gut. These photos will last forever and this dad-bod before I'm a dad has to go... fuck that.

Conversation 16

J.J.M.

Jack James McEwen. There, that's what we've decided to call you, you little rascal. Looking at it now it's the first time I've seen it written down and it's an odd thing to look at in 'print' for the first time. But it looks strong, it looks good, it looks like you – my son x. By the way, if your Mum starts calling you 'JJ' I'm going to change your name to Maximus Decimus Meridius and call you 'Gladiator' for short. Her proclivity for shortening names drives me mental. Well that's the latest, decided just yesterday in fact so I have missed the last 3-4 weeks... the silly season... and before that the big move to your first home.

Let's start there... the move. As you'll come to know in the transient world we now live in moving house is a fucking ball ache wherever you live. It is however a little less stressful here in Dubai where AED 1,500 will get you a miniature army of workers from the sub-continent to pack away, wrap up, disassemble, box up, transport, unwrap, unpack, reassemble and bugger off. Yes, I am aware... I sound like a whiney expat twat. Apologies. I still hate it. There's still work to do and shit to buy as a 1 bed townhouse does not go in to a 3 bed without leaving a few gaps. It'll all come together over the next month or 2 so no need to stress.

A week after all this we were back in England to celebrate your grandad's 70th birthday on Christmas Eve and spend Christmas with you Uncle, Aunty, cousins and Nana. Good times had by all. Cold as fucking brass balls out there in East Anglia but good times. Ate my body weight in turkey, roasties, stuffing, chipolatas, bacon and pork pies – working on this 'Dad bod' look. Fuck that! I'm in the gym kid and training my fat arse off. I've gotta be in good shape before you're born so I'll look half way fit in all them birth photos. Photos last a lifetime on the internet little man! I've even given up beer in January to speed up the process. I've always been one for setting realistic goals and 'dry January' can piss right off.

It wasn't a big drinking holiday (more eating!) as Mum's got you cooking and her family aren't really drinkers. Well, not like my side of the family anyway. However, I did get rat arse drunk on New Year's Eve back here in Dubai after tucking away more than a few glasses of fine red wine with some perfectly prepared ribeye... that's right – at home. You'd be so proud or disgusted. Whatever, I had fun with just me and your Mum. First NYE in the house since I was a teenager I reckon and if I'm honest I really enjoyed it. BTW, the laser show on the Burj Khalifa was total rubbish if you were anywhere but right in front. If you weren't front and centre you might as well have been on the dark side of the bloody moon! Obviously we weren't there but we have clear line of sight to the Burj from the roof... nothing... bollox.

By the way, according to the App of all pregnancy knowledge you're about as big as a corn on the Cobb – week 22. It could be one of them little organic jobs or a GMO beast fit for 'feeding the 5,000' – they're not very specific when it comes to these fruit and veg comparisons (probably the former)... the dramatic change in size is due to the fact we now measure you from head to toe instead of head to coccyx... I think. I'm pretty sure though.

We're off to Dr. Anni on Friday so will have an update for you then. This is pretty much the check where she has a good butchers hook at your organs as they've now got enough fat around them for an accurate assessment. You will be duly informed xxx

Conversation 17

Attitude

Right there Jack (that still sounds fucking weird in my head. You're name makes it all seem a hell of a lot more real – in a fantastic way of course). We had 'THE' scan on the weekend just gone. As described before this is where the doctor gets a good look at you – and she certainly took her time to make sure all was in good order. Brain, kidneys, liver, heart function and sound, cleft pallet... bloody hell! You're in the clear, kid. There were no markers for anything for us to be concerned about. Long may that continue.

BTW, in one of the scans you were giving us a bit of attitude by giving us the middle finger. You cheeky bugger ☺

At the minute Mum is on the case with pre-natal classes. We're due to start them in a few weeks and fuck me... there is some raft of options. Standard pre-natal, hypnobirthing, standard pre-natal plus some hypno, standard pre-natal plus some hypno plus one session of post-birth care and on and on. Apparently pre-natal hypno is the dogs bollox so we're definitely going to be doing that. Jen (Mum's BFF) has already sent us a link to an audio file that we need to start listening to in preparation. Her and Nick did it with Felix and he's the business so it can't hurt to give it a go right? I think it's now a case of what are we going to add on... maybe we should have all of it as between us we probably have only half a fucking clue what to do once we get you back from the hospital. The good news for you is Mum and I are quick learners.

FYI: the house is still a shit tip of a fuckin mess.

Conversation 18

'Nesting' Sucks Balls!

As you know we are in the middle of sorting out the (your!) house and moving from a 1 bed to 3 bed makes it pretty bloody stressful. TBH I've about had a fucking nough. The landscapers have finally finished after a minor cluster fuck with security access BUT, there's still a few problems that need to be sorted. The furniture we ordered a few weeks ago finally arrived last night BUT, the cushion cover is the wrong colour. Fuck! The TV cabinet arrived BUT, no worries on that one – it fits... just. Thank God!

I saw mum typing away furiously last night. Looked like she was smashing out a list of things to do and things to buy and it looked pretty extensive... bollox! Right now I'd just like a day off and not have to do any 'chores' and not have a single thought about how fucking long that list is... and watch some rugby... and drink some beer!

Conversation 18 sounds a bit shit doesn't it... moaning old bastard! Just got off the phone with your Mum and we have some good news... Dah dah daaaaahhhhhhh: Irish has said she'd be interested in a full time live out nanny position with us. You probably don't quite understand but Irish is our cleaner of about 6-8 years. We haven't seen her for a while as she's been away looking after her new born son who's about a year old now. And what you really don't get is she – is – a – fucking – legend! As discussed previously I was expecting us to jump straight in to a live in nanny arrangement but this is a game changer. Mum loves her, I love her, Rusty loves her and I expect her offer means she loves us... oh yes! Maybe she can help me with this fucking ball ache of a chore list ☺

Conversation 19

Hypno! Hypno! Hypno!

You probably won't get the reference 'Hypno, hypno hypno'... google (or whatever it is when you read this journal) 90's dance music – all the cool kids were doing it! I wasn't doing it... I was a boring bastard just drinking regular beer in a regular pub and playing rugby... like a regular 20 something Kiwi boy.

Hypnobirthing. That's what I'm talking about now. We went to our first class the other night and apart from being held on Hump Day (Tuesday) from 6.30pm – 10.00pm and being 3 and a half hours... on fucking hump day it was pretty good. Seriously though, a room full of pregnant woman yawning their heads after 9pm. I think I'll fill out a feedback card.

Never mind the Mums... at 9.30ish the facilitator took us through some relaxation/meditation techniques. Well that was only ever going to go one way. This fucking twat fell asleep twice – woke myself up twice with a not too subtle snort and had the 'falling twitch' where I near enough slapped the shit out of an imaginary mozzie on my leg. Typically, I thought I'd got away with it until the lesson was over and Mum whispered something to the effect of 'dickhead, you were snoring and you woke me from my relaxing meditative Zen state... asshole!' She didn't say 'asshole' but it was implied in her delivery – haha. Thank God no one else heard right... did they fuck. Getting in the elevator to leave we started chatting to a nice Irish lady.

Chat chat chat blah blah blah 'was that you that started snoring?' Ah FFS... there was another couple in between us and them as well!

What I know now after just 1 session of 4 is that I am the second most important in the room and I have a checklist of things to keep to keep an eye on. Up to this point I thought I was going to be about as useful as tits on a bull. But no, I am extremely important to the birthing process and like all good men I am relieved to have list of specific items to manage. The nightmare scenario would have been something like:

Mum: I'm in pain

Me (in my head): where does it hurt... specifically? What would you like me to do... specifically? Shall I get a doctor? Shall I get a nurse? Am I asking you too many questions? Fuck... I'm asking too many questions. Just figure it out Darrell. Use your inner Jedi to solve this fucking problem!

Mum: I'm uncomfortable

Me (in my head): what is uncomfortable... specifically? What position would you like to try... specifically? Where are the pillows? How does this fucking hospital bed remote control work? This AC control panel is different to home (no shit Sherlock) how do I get it to the perfect temperature? What is the perfect temperature?

I'm delighted to tell you that scenarios like the above play out less and less in my head after just one session. I reckon in 4 sessions time I'd be prepared to deliver you myself in the back of an Uber... Uber Black of course.

44

Conversation 20

Pregnant Woman's Crack

Mum has always had a sweet tooth but holy shit! She has been nailing the milk chocolate lately. So much so that when requested to 'grab a bit of milk chocolate' I specifically selected the bag that has individual portions of 3 small chunks in an attempt to at least curb the habit a bit. Because, of course, if you get the standard block you rip the row off and smash it... hmmm, that's wasn't enough – I think I'll rip in to another row. No one will know. You know what? It worked as well! Low and behold I come home from last night and see 2 massive bags of Galaxy milk chocolate in the fridge... What's this I ask? It was a great deal she said. I got a 1.7% discount if I got 3kgs of chocolate (or something like that ☺). #facepalm

Note: treading very, very carefully here... your Mum is a beautiful woman – end of. She does have a habit of putting herself down. She'll say she doesn't do it that often or exclaim 'I'm just realistic, not negative'. She's blissfully unaware of its frequency. The other day we were driving somewhere and I counted at least 8 times (in a 15min journey!) she was getting stuck in to herself... my bum is too big, I have cellulite, I'm going to get a boob job, I'm getting wrinkles around my eyes, fuck – I'm getting old, my belly is so big my pants are rolling over themselves... no shit. You're pregnant. Beautiful and pregnant!

Cooking is out and Deliveroo is in. As you get bigger she gets more uncomfortable and sleeps less so it's hardly surprising she can't be bothered to cook. I think I'm going to have to get a bit of batch cooking in so we can increase the veg and protein intake and reduce the pad Thai and crispy fried beef consumption. There's no guarantee that she still won't hit the Deliveroo App but at least I can provide an option – here's hoping.

You're Mum is a beautiful pregnant woman. I still would. I still do, albeit a little less frequently xxx

We're off to Sri Lanka tonight for 4 nights – babymoon! Yes, it's a real thing. It will be our last holiday as just the 2 of us. The next holiday we have together will quite likely be in October when we go to New Zealand for Grandma's 60th birthday and it'll be 'Table for 3'.

Right, I've got to get off to the exchange to grab about 1.2M Rupees for our 5 day holiday... I'll keep you posted.

Conversation 21

Babymoon

Yes, boy.... Babymoon is an amazing thing! Any excuse to book a holiday. We stayed at a pretty amazing resort / hotel / boutique guest house – not really sure what the hell to call it. Let's call it a 3 bed boutique guest house for want of a better definition. Whatever... it was the fucking bollox! Burj al Arab boasts something like 5 staff for every guest – this place came pretty bloody close.

Arrived at the place via a very slow path through Kandy... I had beer (3-4) and had a sleep. Fear not, I didn't have my first until approximately 12:03pm – I'm not a fucking animal! Mum had a quick read of her trusty Kindle then slept for about 5 hours.

Refreshed, the next morning we had arranged (well, I did fuck all. The boutique boss did it all) a small site seeing tour. Started a bit ropey at the first temple we went to – Mum spunked AED 75 in to a machine that gave us a CD ROM. A CD ROM – are you fucking serious... 1993 called! I don't deal with crowds and I definitely don't deal with people knocking in to me or touching me... get off me you bastard! To be fair, we thought it was something to do with entry. It was so crowded due to some ceremony that we bailed out, took a selfie for proof of attendance then did one... post haste.

Then on to a mountain temple – amazing!

Then lunch – it was a buffet and it was terrible. Mum had a proper strop. Tried to arrange a la carte for her, she took none glance at it: 'this is disgusting'. I thought she was going to take my bottle of beer, smash it on the table, kick me to the floor and stab me in the throat with it – Once Were Warriors style (NZ movie). I never feared for my life really... remember what I said about letting the truth get in the way of a good story ☺

Then the tea plantation – amazing. We bought some tea (guilt purchase) that I expect we will keep for the appropriate amount time before chucking it out having not even broken the seal.

Then home for a rest. I think Mum forgets she is pregnant sometimes (which is a good thing as you're both obviously getting on well) and is shocked when all of a sudden she gets a bit tired in the early afternoon.

We spent the next few days debating whether or not to leave and before we can get some consensus it was like 1pm, I was having a beer and it was too late to arrange anything. We didn't end up leaving until we had booked a mountain top restaurant for dinner, which was incredible.

Then there was ICECREAM-GATE.

For no apparent reason (preggers!?) your Mum became obsessed with going to some fuckin ice cream place she had seen on tripadvisor or some such shit. It didn't work out on our sightseeing day despite her many vague, nondescript and other wise confusing instructions to the driver. Finally she canned the idea, most likely to physical and mental fatigue.

Thank God she did... I wanted to 45 minutes ago but I'll be fucked if I was going to suggest it!

Having a hell of a memory and not being afraid to use it this carried on in to the next day. I said I would talk to the manager, have him find us a driver, come and collect us at the drop of a hat, take us in to Kandy city, buy a fuckin ice-cream and then bring us all the way back. I think she realized what you and I are both thinking... it came up again???!!! #facepalm! I talk a good story kid so don't stress out about we did have a laugh about it... eventually.

It was a great little holiday... we even celebrated our anniversary while there too. We got a small anniversary cake at breakfast – Mum was delighted to be eating cake for breakfast. Not so delighted when we went back for more in the afternoon to be told it was all gone... ALL GONE?! Who the fuck ate our cake – hahahahaha!

According to LAD Bible couples that drink together and I mean have proper sessions, stay together. Me and your Mum are Level 9,000 at that. If I'm honest, I missed having my drinking buddy.

Conversation 22

Baby-Q

Apologies little bro... been a little busy lately. So let's start with the Baby-Q; 1 part baby shower, 1 part BBQ – that way we can include the fellas. It was a pretty decent affair even if most of us were suffering from fantastic hangovers due to Christie and Kieran's leaving brunch. In typical fashion I arrived and went for it on the booze front then came home with Mum... all tucked up in bed by 8pm I believe. Fucking perfect. Yes, of course Mum is a bit gutted that another one of her besties is leaving. We do, however, seem to go to UK a fair bit so not a total disaster.

Emi and Christie were the organizers and did a bloody great job... dudes arrived with tables, plates, salads and a bloody great big lamb on the spit. Even better... they took all that shit away at the end.

Sunday was a fucking disaster at work!

The next day we went for a scan at the doctors. We might as well not have fucking gone. Again, you were hiding behind the placenta. No photos and fuck all on the monitor. We pretty much turned up to book the next appointment.

Shortly after that Daisy and Rai had their wee baby daughter – Mia. We went to see them pretty much the same day (Mia being about 12 hours old). BTW she is fucking beautiful and you now have that to live up to. Good luck mate as she was quiet, slept most of the time, no crying... an absolute dream. Look now, me and your Mum will do our best to provide you with a low stress introduction to the outside – the rest is up to you. Mia is calm... Mia is clever... Mia is chilled... Be like Mia! You'll be BFFs I'm sure. I said to Mum 'Daisy seemed a bit more chatty than normal'. Found out the next day she was tripping off her nut with a heady concoction of pain relief and natural Oxytocin and barely remembered any of the conversation LOL. Don't bother looking that up as I can tell you exactly what it is – the love hormone! I know all about it from our Hypnobirthing classes as I reckon Ana (the instructor) says the word at least once every 7 minutes. If you do the maths that's a fuck load of times each 3.5hr session.

Conversation 23

Moany McMoanerson

Yes, a slightly controversial way to start this conversation. However by your Mum's own admission this is so. Last night at our catch up and final Hypnobirthing class a lady mentioned that she hasn't really felt pregnant up till now at 35 weeks or something. That's pretty much the only thing that stuck in my mind from the whole 3.5 hours as it seems like that for us. Mum has had such a nice and enjoyable pregnancy I wasn't quite ready for this part. Mum's a bit of a full time resident in 'Struggle Town' populated by other women around the same term. Struggling to sit up, struggling to get up, and struggling to get a night of kip. The struggle is real AF.

I have to admit it's starting to look fucking uncomfortable and there's still 5 weeks to go. Every time she sees her reflection a rather brash tirade of 'fat this, fat that, fuck this fucking fat shit!' occurs. The current obsession is with her ankles... all swollen from fluid retention. Seriously, every time we sit down she takes a butchers at her ankles and huffs and puffs. She was even scanning the room last night looking at every single women's ankles just to check if anyone else was suffering with the same affliction. I'm no fucking help on that front either. I think all feet are fucking minging. I look at all feet and all I see is that Frodo Baggins' fucking trotters – urgh! However, I did buy a bucket and some bath salts and prepared Mum a foot bath last week. I reckon I'm going to have to go one step further, take one for the team and massage her trotters... I'll keep you posted.

Conversation 24

'They'

Whoever 'they' are I wish they would fuck right off!

Mum has been starting pretty much every pregnancy and birth related conversation with 'they' say this or 'they' say that. I don't know who 'they' are and I don't know what 'they' want. What I do have is a particular personality trait where I don't fucking care about your non-medical, unsubstantiated stupid fucking opinion. If you delete your dumb arse opinion posts in your usual Facebook secret society, illuminati Mum groups that'll be the end of it. That goes for you fucking bloggers too!

Like being a first time mother isn't confusing enough. I work in fitness and I've heard as many 'experts' talking about the placenta as I have fucktard fitness 'influencers' talking about the best ways to 'feel the fucking burn!' Piss off!

'They' say post-natal depression starts on 'x' day after birth.

'They' say the nursery should be this colour or that colour for development.

'They' say this is good for your nipples.

'They' say that drinking tea sprinkled with the dehydrated dust of a woodland pixeys sleep bogie is great for bloody well everything'

You know who else knows... the doctor. You know another person that knows... Ana, the doula who taught the hypno class. You know why? Because they're educated. Because their education is fact based and peer reviewed. Because they're experienced. Because they've delivered or supported the delivery of 1,000s of babies.

Disclaimer 1:

A single digit percentage of 'their' information has been helpful. The rest appears to be attention seeking, 'like' grabbing, narcissistic twits.

Disclaimer 2: this is not a 'go' at Mum. Of course she wants as much information and advice as possible. It makes sense to gather information. The trouble is, it is often the negative experiences read about that entrench themselves in the brain. Sadly, an all too common human personality trait. As I was taught in hypno I have been furiously trying to block these negatives – the struggle is real and it continues.

Now I know what it's like for first time gym goers with all the distraction of conflicting information from fitness 'experts, influencers, bloggers' and wellness wank puffins all competing for 'likes', love, shares, comments and anything else their social media accounts can provide for their flailing egos.

Disclaimer 3: I have a lot of time for social media personalities/pages as long they are measured, experienced & educated in their respective fields. I actually follow some... and comment... sometimes.

No more disclaimers; if anyone gives you shit about, or are offended by such comments simply tell them to shut the fuck up and get on with their life... mamby pamby #snowflake. If you decide to categorise yourself as an 'influencer' #sorrynotsorry #lol #mylifemyrules #like #ohmyfcuk

Also; I think the film 'Taken' will still be fucking epic in 10 or so years when you watch it... on your holographic TV... or your contact lens projection system.

Conversation 25

Easy Does It

This is it kid... the last written conversation before we get to meet you in all your chubby, hairy glory. We know this to be true as at your last scan the doctor was pissing herself laughing at the site of your little fat rolls on the back of your neck as well as clearly visible hair floating in the fluid around you. At least we got a decent scan of you this time... you little bugger!

Your due date is 2 weeks from now and could really come any time between now and then or perhaps even a little after. I think I already said that I agreed to allow Mum to read these conversations only once she was in the hospital hence this being the last entry so I can get it to someone to proof read it (hopefully your Grandad Mark as he's a bloody clever chap and I reckon he'll get it done quick smart).

Mum and I went to dinner last night at Maine and it dawned on us that this might be the last time we go out to dinner at a restaurant as part of a 2 person family. I know, it's pretty fucking stupid with all these realisations or milestones that we come with... 'the last time this...' 'the last time that...' twats! I make no apologies.

The 'hospital bag' has quickly turned in to the 'hospital suitcase' FFS. There's a few more things I might have to nip and get this afternoon but we're pretty much done and ready – well, as ready as we'll ever fucking well be. Oh, no... there is the matter of your outfits for the hospital. I promise I will never refer to what you wear as an 'outfit' hence forth. It's called 'getting dressed' not trying to put together an 'outfit'. Right yeah, Mum didn't like any of your clothes (you have quite a few!) and has decided you need something extra special so she needs to go out and buy some... buggered if I'm making those decisions as I'd just cock it up.

So next stop is your birth. Go easy on your Mum, she's done such a brilliant job of getting you to this point. I'm so proud of her and the way she has got on with her pregnancy – even enjoyed it. I don't need you fucking it up at the last hurdle. Easy does it Jack.

If I decide to write 'Volume II' I will detail the birth to you as I'm sure there will be a few stories to tell.

Jack. I am your Father. I love you.

Dad xxx

Printed in Great Britain
by Amazon